Native American Biographies

DENNIS BANKS

NATIVE AMERICAN ACTIVIST

Kae Cheatham

E **Enslow Publishers, Inc.**

44 Fadem Road	PO Box 38
Box 699	Aldershot
Springfield, NJ 07081	Hants GU12 6BP
USA	UK

Library of Congress Cataloging-in-Publication Data

Cheatham, Kae.
    Dennis Banks: Native American activist / Kae Cheatham.
      p. cm. — (Native American biographies)
    Includes bibliographical references and index.
    Summary: Profiles the life and work of the man who founded the
American Indian Movement (AIM) in 1968 in order to protect the rights of
Native Americans.
    ISBN 0-89490-869-3
    1. Banks, Dennis—Juvenile literature. 2. American Indian Movement—
Juvenile literature. 3. Ojibwa Indians—Biography—Juvenile literature.
4. Indians of North America—Government relations—Juvenile literature.
[1. Banks, Dennis. 2. Ojibwa Indians—Biography. 3. Indians of North
America—Biography. 4. American Indian Movement.] I. Title II. Series
E99.C6B263 1997
305.897'073'092—dc21
    [B]   96-39560
                                              CIP
                                              AC

Printed in the United States of America

10 9 8 7 6 5 4 3 2 1

Photo Credits: ©1996 Star Tribune/Minneapolis-St. Paul, p. 32;
AKWESASNE NOTES, Mohawk Nation, p. 45; AKWESASNE NOTES, Vol.
6, No. 4, Mohawk Nation, p. 71; AKWESASNE NOTES, Vol. 18, No. 5,
Mohawk Nation, p. 82; Alice Lambert-Banks, p. 93; © Michelle Vignes,
pp. 4, 68; Paul Stafford, © Minnesota Office of Tourism, pp. 11, 16;
Reprinted with permission of Tribune Media Services, p. 63; Sandy
Solomon/NYT Pictures, p. 77; SunSpot/Kae Cheatham, pp. 26, 49;
UPI/BETTMAN, pp. 43, 72.

Cover Photo: Stephanie Lam-Wong

❄➤ CONTENTS ◄❄

Dennis Banks

IN CUSTER

Wesley Bad Heart Bull, a member of the Lakota Sioux Nation, was dead. The twenty-year-old Native American died from stab wounds he received on January 21, 1973, outside a bar in Buffalo Gap, South Dakota. The white man who killed him, Darold Schmidt, posted a five thousand dollar bond and was released on bail. The next week, Darold Schmidt pleaded guilty to second-degree manslaughter, and the court put him on probation. He did not go to jail.

❖AIM Steps In❖

Wesley Bad Heart Bull's mother, Sarah, wanted murder charges brought against Schmidt. She wrote to the Custer County district attorney. When she did this, she also asked for support from the American Indian Movement (AIM), a national activist organization started in 1968. Dennis Banks is its founding member.

Banks and other AIM members talked to Sarah Bad Heart Bull and agreed to help her. They arranged a meeting between Dennis Banks, Lakota leaders, and state's attorney Hobart Gates. The meeting would be on February 6, 1973.

❖Banks and AIM❖

Dennis Banks is a Leech Lake Anishinabe who was in his early forties in the 1970s. His involvement was not uncommon in situations such as these. He had started the American Indian Movement in 1968 to see that Native Americans received fair treatment by the police and the legal system in Minneapolis, Minnesota. The goals of AIM quickly expanded to include protecting the rights of Native Americans all over the country. At the time of the Bad Heart Bull killing, AIM was one of several organizations that addressed the problems of Native American rights. Many groups had developed in urban areas with large communities of Native Americans. The 1970 census reported that nearly 45 percent of Native Americans in the United States lived in metropolitan areas.[1]

❖Native American Concerns❖

In 1973, AIM was a new Native American organization compared to many other groups. Native American reservations throughout the country had active organizations. The United Sioux Tribes, for example, was formed in 1963. This group worked to improve the image of the Lakota Nation and to promote unity among its people. For decades, Native American communities in the Southwest had battled to keep real estate, utility, and mining companies from taking over their land. In the Pacific Northwest and Great Lakes regions, reservation residents also had many concerns. The American Indian Movement was an urban organization. By 1973, its membership included Native American students, workers, scholars, and prisoners, from urban areas and from reservations. They came from many different tribal groups and nations.

Dennis Banks and AIM leaders demanded that Native American communities be in control of their own tribal policies so that they would not have to wait for decisions by the state and federal governments. Equality before the law was very important, too. Dennis Banks and AIM felt that the courts often treated Native Americans more harshly than whites. The fact that Darold Schmidt served no jail time for killing Wesley Bad Heart Bull encouraged AIM's involvement in this case.

❖Conflict in Custer❖

Dennis Banks arrived at the historic courthouse in Custer, South Dakota, on February 6, 1973. Local police and state troopers were already at the scene. Sarah Bad Heart Bull and other people gathered in the falling snow outside the building. Many of them lived on the Pine Ridge Reservation about fifty miles away. Other supporters traveled from the Rosebud Reservation farther east, or from nearby Rapid City, South Dakota. As the meeting progressed, the number of supporters swelled to nearly two hundred. More law enforcement officials showed up. Distrust on both sides grew, and violence erupted.

For the town of Custer, the afternoon clash between white officials and Native Americans was a horrible event. For Dennis Banks, that day in Custer greatly affected the rest of his life.

BEGINNINGS

Dennis James Banks has a forceful voice and kind eyes. He grew up under circumstances very different from the average American. He was born April 12, 1932, on the Leech Lake Reservation, in north-central Minnesota. Leech Lake is home to one group of Anishinabe. Their name means "first man." Hundreds of years ago, their neighbors called them Ojibwa. When white trappers arrived, they misnamed them Chippewa.

❖The Anishinabe People❖

Historically, the Anishinabe homeland ranged from the shores of four of the five Great Lakes (Erie, Huron, Michigan, and Superior). It stretched across what is now southern Canada and the states of Wisconsin and Minnesota, all the way to the Turtle Mountain region of North Dakota. Their traditional lifestyle included hunting, trapping, and especially fishing in the lakes and streams. They also harvested wild rice. These activities are still important to the Anishinabe lifestyle today. Their traditional lodges were most often constructed from bark and matting of the great forest trees. The material was overlapped like large shingles. This kept the rain and snow out of the dwelling.

❖Reservations are Formed❖

After the War of 1812, those Anishinabe who lived south of the Great Lakes and Canadian border agreed to a treaty with the United States government. Signed in 1815, the treaty protected from white intrusion Native American lands in northern Michigan, Wisconsin, Minnesota, and North Dakota. Reservations represent the largest form of the Native American land base.

In the early nineteenth century, the secretary of war created the Office of Indian Affairs. It is now called the Bureau of Indian Affairs (BIA). The BIA oversees most of the activities on reservations,

— ❖ —

The Anishinabe land where Dennis Banks was born is shown here.

including the sale and lease of lands and the welfare of reservation inhabitants. Dennis Banks has been very outspoken about the BIA. This government agency, according to Banks, has done more to hurt Native American communities than to help them.

Today, Native American reservation land makes up some 84,375 of this country's 3,548,000 square miles of land, which is a total of about 2.4 percent. About 35 percent of the Native American population lives on this reservation land.[1]

Leech Lake Reservation, of Dennis Banks's birth, was established in 1855. It contains 600,000 acres of land, but the Anishinabe live on only 27,853 acres. It is a joint-use reservation: The other 572,000 acres make up parks, fishing lakes, and hiking trails, open to the public.[2]

❖Education on the Reservation❖

In the 1930s, many Native American children received their education at BIA boarding schools. Often Catholic, Lutheran, or other churches controlled these schools. The government operated the rest of them. In 1933, when Dennis Banks was just one year old, the new Commissioner of Indian Affairs, John Collier, made important changes in the BIA. The school system was one of those changes. Collier encouraged school officials to teach classes in the native language of the students, as well as in English. This system of instruction is called bilingual education. Collier began training programs for the teachers. The schools were still run mostly by white people, however. It was not until 1969 that Native Americans could finally participate in what and how their children learned.

Today, many reservations have day schools. The BIA still operates over two hundred schools. All of them now have Native American teachers and officials. In many regions, children attend public schools in nearby towns. When Dennis Banks was young, children often had to travel to schools in states different from where they lived. They did not see their families for several months, sometimes years.

❖Banks Goes to Boarding School❖

Dennis Banks's first boarding school was four hundred miles from his home. He was sent there when he was five years old. Banks later described this schooling as "trying to destroy the very structure of Indian society."[3]

In boarding schools, the children were forbidden to speak their own language or have any traditional ceremonies. If they tried, they were often whipped. Sometimes students were tied to their beds or closed in a dark room alone.

The government school in Wahpeton, North Dakota, was 170 miles from Leech Lake. Young students there had their hair cut short, were stripped, covered with an insecticide, and sent to take showers. After the shower, if they did not seem clean enough, they received hard whacks with a wooden ruler. Then they were sent back into the showers. These harsh conditions continued during studies. Corporal punishment (punishment to one's body) was the usual means of correction. Students often tried to run away from these schools. School officials worked hard to keep students there. After a few years, students usually forgot their native language. They began to think of their culture as shameful. For some, like Dennis Banks, however, a bud of resentment remained throughout their life. This resentment later encouraged Banks to become active in helping other Native Americans.

Banks attended boarding schools throughout his education. In 1953 he enlisted in the United States Air Force and served a tour of duty in Japan. A different attitude by the government toward Native Americans began while he was out of the United States. During the 1880s, the government had worked very hard to force Native Americans to live and believe the way most white people did. This policy was called assimilation. In the 1930s, more effort had been made to let Native Americans be themselves. In the 1950s, however, the government went back to thinking that Native Americans should be like everyone else.

❖Relocation Programs❖

In 1952, the government's Voluntary Relocation Program encouraged Native Americans to leave their reservation lands. They were persuaded to settle in urban areas. Major cities had relocation centers where counseling and assistance offered promises of a better life. Congress passed the Termination Resolution in 1953. This allowed certain states to handle the legal problems on reservations without the consent of tribal governments. The next decade resulted in changes in the management of health care for Native Americans. Federal recognition for more than fifty tribes and Native American communities was denied.

The relocation and termination programs did not produce the successes the government expected. Native American communities attempted various businesses. Most businesses failed because the Native Americans had little money and business expertise. Reservation land that had been owned by the Native American government was divided up between individual families on the reservation. Many Native Americans were uninformed and undereducated. They had no government protection. The communities lost their land to taxes and land swindles. In many cities, the relocation program merely created new ghettos. Minneapolis, the site of one of the first relocation centers, now has one of the country's largest Native American populations.

In 1958, Dennis Banks ended his service with the air force. He returned to the United States and to Native American communities that were very discouraged. Upon his discharge, he became just another urban Native American who could not find steady employment. He became a drifter and ". . . bummed around between the reservation and Minneapolis and St. Paul. . . . There were no jobs, nothing."[4]

Banks got in trouble with the law. In 1966, he was arrested and convicted of burglary. He received a five-year sentence at the Minnesota State Prison in Stillwater.

"When I got to prison . . . I finally began to understand the word 'discrimination.' I wanted to

— ◈ —

The skyline of Minneapolis, Minnesota, site of a large Native American relocation center and the place where Dennis Banks and others founded the American Indian Movement (AIM) is shown here.

challenge it. . . . I came out of prison in 1968 determined to build a new road for my life."[5]

While in prison, Dennis Banks read *Black Elk Speaks*. This book contains the written words of Oglala spiritual leader Black Elk. They were recorded by John Niehardt in 1932. The book describes the daily, cultural, and spiritual life of the Lakota in the late 1800s. It also speaks about the relationship the Lakota had with the government. Banks said, "I really began to think about treaty rights, civil rights, human rights."[6]

Banks was paroled from Stillwater in 1968. He had served twenty-eight months of his sentence. He got a job with the Honeywell Corporation, and he sought out Clyde Bellecourt. Bellecourt had been in prison when Banks was there. Banks joined Bellecourt and George Mitchell in a series of meetings in Minneapolis. Serious problems existed in the city due to racism and discrimination against Native Americans. The school dropout rate and the number of Native American arrests were very high. At the meetings, Banks and Bellecourt discussed ways to change these statistics. In July 1968, more than two hundred fifty people showed up at a meeting. According to Banks, "That was the beginning of AIM."[7]

Coast to Coast

At first, Dennis Banks and the others considered calling their new social rights group the Concerned Indian Americans. They decided against that. They did not want to use the letters C.I.A. as their organization's initials. Pat Ballenger, considered the mother of the movement, suggested A.I.M.—American Indian Movement.[1] So AIM it was.

◈Cultural Awareness Awakens◈

Throughout the late 1950s and into the 1960s, in Washington state, Wisconsin, and Michigan,

Native Americans—including the Anishinabe of Banks's heritage—participated in fish-ins to demonstrate against lost fishing rights. They also protested environmental problems that were affecting the fish population they counted on for food. The fish-ins were similar to the sit-ins of the civil rights movement. Native Americans would go to the disputed fishing sites and begin fishing, or just remain there, until law officers made them move. These fish-ins led to numerous arrests, violence, and even Native American deaths.

The fish-ins and sit-ins were part of the social change happening in every part of the United States. The Women's Liberation Movement was growing. By the late 1960s, demonstrations concerning the United States' involvement in the war in southeast Asia were common. Many demonstrations took place at colleges and universities. At this same time, African-American, Hispanic-American and Native American students began insisting on course curricula that included more information about their cultures. Often the demands led to activities that resulted in property destruction, clashes with police, and many arrests. There were fish-ins, sit-ins, and teach-ins, and the popular term of the day was power. Along with Black Power there was Chicano Power; Flower Power for the antiwar movement; Green Power for the environmental movement; and Red Power for the new Native American movement, in which Dennis Banks was involved.

❖Red Power and AIM❖

Lakota scholar and former director of the National Congress of American Indians (NCAI), Vine Deloria, Jr., was one of the first to use the term *Red Power*. "In 1966 [we used it] as a means of putting the establishment on. We were greatly surprised when newspapermen began to take us seriously . . .,"[2] Deloria, Jr., said. "The concept of power. . . . meant that the group could speak and demand as a group."[3]

Red Power organizations were beginning in Native American communities all over the country. Urban and rural people became interested in finding out about their culture and their political rights. The interest spread to colleges and universities, too. The declaration of purpose was written in 1969 by university students and community members in Ann Arbor, Michigan. The first paragraph reads:

> *We, the members of the American Indians Unlimited, have organized to remove the myth of the "vanishing American." Although prejudice and poverty have placed the American Indian behind the American Scene, we intend to demonstrate that American Indians are an integral part of this society, with a voice, a culture, and the right to share fully in this democratic system.*[4]

This was very similar to the goals of many other organizations, including AIM. During its first year,

AIM concentrated on increasing employment opportunities, getting better housing, and improving education in Minneapolis-St. Paul, Minnesota. There, large communities of low-income Native Americans lived in poor conditions. High unemployment and school dropout rates were common. Dennis Banks had completed his basic education. He recognized the importance of staying in school. He read books and knew how to make people listen when he spoke. He also knew that education was very important for the young Native Americans of Minneapolis.

Even today, when compared to the rest of the nation, Native Americans have the highest infant mortality rate, the shortest life span of any ethnic group, the lowest income per-capita, and the highest suicide rate. There are more school dropouts among Native Americans than any other group. Most Native Americans experience the poorest housing conditions and the highest unemployment of any group of people in the country.[5]

◈AIM in Minneapolis◈

Banks and other AIM leaders realized that the work to improve education and employment was not enough. In Minneapolis-St. Paul, a large number of police arrests occurred among the Native American population. Dennis Banks had been arrested. He knew what the process was like.

In order to protect other Native Americans, Banks and AIM leaders organized street patrols. Young men and women, wearing red jackets and berets, monitored police activities. They carried tape recorders, two-way radios, and cameras. Often they followed police cars or showed up at crime scenes to film arrests. They gave advice to those arrested concerning their rights.

The patrols resulted in fewer Native American arrests. More humane treatment was given to those who were arrested. These activities received national attention. Eventually, AIM began receiving support from businesses, churches, and civic groups. AIM was becoming a powerful organization in the forefront of the struggle for Native American rights.

Banks wanted to do more. He began running classes to tell young people about the destructive powers of alcohol and drugs. He often helped people get into alcohol rehabilitation programs. Through his job as a recruiter for the Honeywell Corporation, he helped to find employment opportunities for others. The American Indian Movement also began helping people adjust to the urban society, without losing the important parts of their own Native American culture.

❖AIM and Native American Culture❖

When many Africans were brought to this land against their will and forced into slavery, they lost most of their cultural heritage. European and Asian immigrants most often came here willingly and maintained some of their overseas roots. Native Americans, however, still exist in the original place of their ancestors. Their culture is connected with the land, and the land is part of who they are.

This history created a different set of goals for Dennis Banks and other Native American activists of the 1970s. Native Americans have never wanted to forget or give up who they are. Treaty rights and Native American sovereignty (independence) became important issues. Native Americans wanted control over how their land would be handled. They wanted their laws and beliefs as a people to be recognized.

"The lines are not AIM and the Bureau of Indian Affairs," wrote Helen Peterson, an Oglala AIM member from Pine Ridge who has held several top positions with the BIA, the NCAI, and other social-relations organizations. ". . . [T]he thing that needs to be understood above and beyond all else, is that . . . land is what is at the bottom of all of it. It has been for almost five hundred years."[6]

❖Banks Seizes Alcatraz❖

In November 1969, fourteen Native Americans "repossessed" the deserted prison island of Alcatraz in San Francisco Bay. Dennis Banks was among those who landed boats on the shores of Alcatraz Island. He and other activists hoped to bring attention to the poverty, poor housing, and lack of education with which most Native people lived. They thought of the remote and neglected Alcatraz Island in the same way as the reservations. They cited treaty rights that guaranteed the return of unoccupied federal land to Native Americans.

Within days, nearly one hundred Native Americans occupied the houses where the guards had lived and the empty cement block buildings of the prison. "Alcatraz Is Indian Country" said one of the signs that hung from the walls. The population on the island often changed. Some people stayed for months, others stayed for only a week or so at a time. Banks moved on to other activities. Yet the occupation proceeded through the winter of 1969. In all, it lasted nineteen months, until June 1971. During that time, a cultural school helped many urban Native Americans to reconnect with their culture and tribal heritage. Negotiations and meetings between the Alcatraz leadership and the government did not produce anything positive, but the media attention did. Red Power, Dennis Banks, and AIM recognized a new way to let the public know about problems in the Native American community.

❖Red Power Spreads❖

Takeover of government land began all across the country. In many places, the takeovers were led by AIM members. In 1970 and again in 1971, for example, a group of Oglala from South Dakota's Pine Ridge Reservation encamped on Mount Rushmore to protest what they considered a desecration of the Black Hills. They believe the government stole this sacred land from them. Members of AIM who lived in the area participated in this protest. They were led by an Oglala woman in her seventies.

In March 1970, in the fifth month of the Alcatraz occupation, thirty Native Americans attempted to seize Ellis Island, near Jersey City, New Jersey. The leaders of the group hoped that taking Ellis Island

— ◆ —

Many Oglala people believe that these carved faces of United States Presidents at Mount Rushmore are a desecration of their sacred Black Hills.

would unite the Red Power movement from both coasts. *The New York Times* reported John White Fox, a Shoshone leader, as saying, "It's time for my people to stand up, to live a little."[7]

At the time of the Ellis Island attempt, Native Americans also staged a sit-in at the BIA office in Littleton, Colorado. This came after a formal complaint of job discrimination had been filed against the BIA and a local Littleton industry. The National Indian Youth Council (NIYC) filed the initial complaint. Support for the sit-in came from Banks and AIM of Minneapolis. After three days, police emptied the building of activists and arrested twelve people. They became known as the Littleton Twelve. On March 26, 1970, the NIYC put out a news release regarding the situation. It stated:

> When . . . the arrests were reported in the national press a wave of demonstrations were set off around the country. . . . in support of what has now become known as the "Littleton Twelve."
>
> [In another demonstration] [i]n Minneapolis, Minnesota, the American Indian Movement (AIM) under the direction of Clyde Bellecourt and Dennis Banks is currently sustaining a demonstration of 100 Indian people at the BIA installation there.
>
> Already the movement in support of the "Littleton Twelve" . . . has grown to several thousand Indian people from both urban areas and reservations.[8]

Dennis Banks and eleven other AIM members were arrested. They were charged with trespassing for their part in the Minneapolis sit-in. They all pleaded innocent and requested a jury trial. The next year, BIA officials said they did not want to prosecute and dropped all charges.

Littleton, Mount Rushmore, Ellis Island, and Alcatraz were not isolated incidents. All across the country, demonstrations and formal petitions to the government were common. Meanwhile, membership in AIM continued to grow. Large AIM chapters developed in Cleveland, Ohio; Denver, Colorado; Chicago, Illinois; and San Francisco, California.

A common style of dress and accessories became popular among these new activists. They adopted jeans and Western boots or moccasins. Men and women wore their hair long, either streaming loose or in braids. In those days, Banks most often wore a headband. Many people wore beaded items. The white communities near reservations often mistook the pride shown by these people for hostility. AIM also adopted a practice of flying the American flag upside down. This brought more criticism and anger, because an upside-down flag is an international distress signal. While Banks and AIM supporters considered it a fitting display of their situation, others did not.

❖Entertainment Protests❖

In 1970, Dennis Banks and AIM received more national attention. Members across the country boycotted the movie *A Man Called Horse*. The boycott protested the continual degradation of Native American culture in Hollywood films. Native American communities also disliked the fact that Native American actors were rarely used to play the parts of Native Americans.

In July, Banks and six other AIM members accepted an invitation by the Michigan-based Great Lakes Indian Youth Alliance (GLIYA) to help in a protest. A play there told about the arrival of a Catholic priest, Federic Baraga, and fur traders to the Upper Peninsula of Michigan. Many Anishinabe and members of the local Keewenau Bay Tribal Council felt the play portrayed their people as cruel, ignorant, and savage.[9] A misunderstanding between pageant officials and demonstrators led to some pushing and name-calling. The Saturday performance was canceled. One person was arrested.

On Sunday, the show went on. After the performance, Dennis Banks gained permission to speak to the audience. In intense, yet reasonable tones, he said that the demonstrators had not wanted to stop the pageant. However, he felt the audience should know the true story about the mistreatment of Michigan's Native Americans. "Missionaries played a major role in having these people . . . sign away thousands and thousands of acres," Banks said.[10]

❖Social and Educational Goals❖

Dennis Banks and the AIM leadership always maintained traditional Native American values. This helped the relationship AIM members had with tribal elders and full-bloods. Full-bloods are those people who have only Native American ancestry. They often do not trust urban people and ideas. On some of the reservations in the West, tribal elders began to unite with the vocal younger people. They were glad to see them wanting to learn more about their heritage.

Government policies toward Native Americans had changed yet again. The relocation and termination programs that had started in the 1950s were pushed aside. The government began helping Native American organizations with their programs. This allowed Banks and other AIM leaders to realize one of their major goals. In 1971, with government funding, AIM opened their first Native People's Survival School, located in Minneapolis, Minnesota. This school became an alternative to reform school for juvenile offenders. By the end of 1972, AIM had established two more schools.

In 1972, a new national AIM office opened in Washington, D.C. Dennis Banks was one of the directors. This East Coast location did not keep Banks from involvement in issues at home, however. Working with the Minneapolis African-American community, Banks and other AIM members helped found the Legal Rights Center.

❖Banks Is Charged with Trespassing❖

Not long after the dismissal of the Minneapolis BIA trespassing charges, Dennis Banks was again charged with trespassing. He had organized a five-day AIM occupation of the abandoned Twin Cities Naval Air Station; he and nearly seventy other Native Americans claimed the unused base. Many were women and children. They took a gas-powered generator to the base because there was no electricity. They also set up a school and began holding first aid classes.

On May 21, fifty-one United States marshals with riot sticks and thirty-four local sheriff's deputies came to the base. They told the people to leave. Some did, but Banks and twenty-seven other AIM members were forcibly removed from the base. Banks was one of fourteen people charged with trespassing. Two others were charged with assault, and the rest were let go.[11] Banks later discussed the situation with Minnesota Senator Walter Mondale. The two men also talked about the need for more control by Native Americans over their own social welfare.

❖Banks as a Forceful Speaker❖

Dennis Banks's ability to communicate and speak before groups was always very important. Monetary donations kept the AIM offices running. Banks often traveled around the country to gain support from tribal groups. He also raised money for upcoming

— ◆ —

Dennis Banks is shown here (left) explaining the grievances of local Native Americans to Minnesota Senator Walter Mondale.

projects. A fund was established to cover the legal costs for AIM members who were arrested at demonstrations. National churches and community rights organizations helped support these efforts.

Banks stressed the need for the government to uphold treaty rights. He continued to speak out against alcohol and drug use. He spoke of the need to recommit to the Native American identity. Many people heard the message he spread with his direct way of speaking. He often worked out of California. He made friends with many Hollywood movie stars who supported civil and cultural rights. Some of these people would be important in Banks's later legal battles.

Banks also spoke to Native Americans. In 1972, AIM had a spring organizational meeting in Leech Lake, Minnesota. Banks told AIM chapter leaders from around the country that no one was going to take them seriously if the Movement did not conduct itself in a serious manner. Banks constantly discouraged the use of alcohol and drugs. At first, Banks's insistence caused some friction within the organization. Herb Prowless, however, leader of the AIM chapter in Milwaukee, Wisconsin, backed Banks, as did many others.

Banks traveled to Florida in 1972. There he confronted the president's daughter, Julie Nixon Eisenhower, in Miami. She was attending the Republican National Convention. Banks spoke to her about the conditions under which Native Americans lived. He gave her a list of demands about Native American education and housing. He wanted President Richard Nixon to see the list.

AIM continued to use non-violent tactics and sit-ins to get their message across. In 1972, however, violent political clashes occurred in parts of Europe, Africa, and Asia. In Munich, Germany, during the 1972 Olympic Games, Middle-Eastern terrorists invaded the Olympic village and killed twelve Israeli athletes. The United States experienced violence, too. The 1968 assassinations of Martin Luther King, Jr. and Robert Kennedy were just a few examples. Banks and AIM, however, did not use these types of actions to make their point.

❖ 1972 National Meeting ❖

AIM national meetings often took place in regions of the country that had economic or racial problems. Sometimes AIM members were able to start a dialogue between Native Americans and members of white communities. The 1972 AIM National Council meeting took place on August 7 on the Pine Ridge Reservation in South Dakota.

Pine Ridge, established in 1868, consists of 1,780,444 acres of land. It is the second most populated reservation in the country.[12] The eleven thousand Oglalas who lived on this reservation are some of the poorest people in the country.

Many of the Oglala elders at Pine Ridge felt the BIA did not fairly represent them. AIM began to support the protests of these dissatisfied Oglalas. The presence of AIM in South Dakota would also have an impact on Banks's life.

❖Sun Dance❖

Later that month, on the Rosebud Reservation in south-central South Dakota, several AIM members took part in the annual Sun Dance. The Sun Dance is an important religious ceremony for Native Americans of the Plains. It is also a time of reflection, sacrifice, and commitment to personal goals. It involves continuous dancing without food or water. Gazing toward the sun during the four-day event is a means toward purification of the soul. Some participants pierce their breast muscles with skewers of wood, then suspend themselves by these skewers from the special Sun Dance pole, which has been blessed by the holy men.

In the nineteenth century, the United States government forbade the Sun Dance. Native Americans were forced to perform the Sun Dance in secret. If they were caught, participants were arrested. In 1936 the government removed the ban, and the ceremony has since been held every year.

At the 1972 Sun Dance, a discussion developed about the failures of the government to deal with Native American problems. Someone suggested,

"Maybe we should do something like the civil rights movement's 1963 March on Washington."[13]

✦Planning the March on Washington, D.C.✦

A month later, many of these same people met with others in Denver, Colorado. They began organizing a march on Washington, D.C. The meeting atmosphere was one of deep concern. Just one week earlier, Richard Oakes, a Mohawk activist who had started the Indian studies programs in California schools, had been killed by a white man near his home. Oakes and Dennis Banks had worked together during the Alcatraz occupation. No one was ever charged in connection with his death.

After three days of meetings, the leaders had developed a list of twenty major problems in Native American communities throughout North America. Many of these "Twenty Points" stressed the need for more self-government in Native American communities. These were the same points for which Dennis Banks and AIM leaders had always pressed. The leaders also felt that government officials should give less consideration to the natural resources on tribally owned land and more to Native American rights.

Letters were exchanged with the White House. The planned event became known as the Trail of Broken Treaties Caravan. It was a combined effort of many organizations, including the Native American

Rights Fund and the National Indian Brotherhood (of Canada). The National Indian Lutheran Board, the United Native Americans, and other groups also supported the Twenty Points.

"Each trail will be led by spiritual leaders who will carry the Sacred Peace Pipe and Drum," reported a statement from the group. "Every drum will beat day and night, reminding Americans of the treaties; and every peace pipe smoked will remind America and history of the manner under which the treaties were signed."[14]

The first trail leader was Robert Burnette from the Rosebud Reservation. However, Dennis Banks and other AIM members soon became important members of this caravan. This was the beginning of a national demonstration. It expressed many of the goals with which Banks had concerned himself for five years. Unfortunately, things would not develop the way demonstration leaders hoped.

CONFRONTATIONS

On October 6, 1972, Dennis Banks led more than fifty cars from San Francisco, California, headed toward St. Paul, Minnesota, where they would join Trails travelers from the Midwest. Other official groups were leaving from Los Angeles, California, and Seattle, Washington. One group from the West went through Oklahoma and followed the Cherokee Trail of Tears. Crossing historic locales and offering prayers for the living and the dead was an integral part of the plan. Americans needed to be reminded of the problems facing Native Americans throughout the country.

Banks took his group through the Black Hills of South Dakota, where they stopped at the small village of Wounded Knee. Wounded Knee is the place where the United States Army killed Black Kettle and his Lakota people, mostly women and children, in 1890. The mass grave, where army officials dumped the three hundred bodies, remains at that site. Banks and his group held a ceremonial service there with the Lakota people who were joining the caravan.

The number of protesters grew as the caravan continued to move toward Washington, D.C. A spiritual and peaceful nature was intended for the entire demonstration—liquor and drugs were forbidden. Spiritual leaders accompanied each group of travelers. When the groups reached Washington, D.C., they intended to have a ceremony at Arlington National Cemetery, at the graves of two Native American World War II veterans. One of the soldiers, John Rice, a Lakota, had been killed during the Korean War. He was buried in Arlington by order of President Harry S. Truman. Memorial Park, a cemetery in Sioux City, Iowa, had refused the service.

❖The Mood Changes❖

The groups reached Washington, D.C., early on the morning of November 2, 1972. Dennis Banks led the first arrivals. The line of cars and buses carrying the protesters stretched out for four miles.

There were problems, however. Government officials, who had earlier said they would cooperate, now refused to communicate with group leaders. Expected housing was no longer available. An abandoned church was offered for lodging, but it had rats and roaches in the basement, and there was no heat. Leadership did not think the place was suitable. There were many children and elderly among the travelers.

Banks took his group to the BIA office to speak with officials about housing. Soon, several hundred people rested in the BIA auditorium and on the lawn outside. Group leaders tried to find a solution to the housing situation. Meanwhile, more protesters were still arriving in Washington. As the afternoon wore on, the Native Americans settled into the BIA building. They refused to be turned out. They had nowhere else to go; "occupation" began.

Banks headed up security and internal operations. Child care was arranged and the elderly were made comfortable. The government protested and sent guards to surround the building. The army canceled the intended ceremonies at the national cemetery, upsetting many people. Eventually, a group of guards entered the building and began forcing people outside. The guards used clubs, and some of the caravan members tried to protect themselves. Other people panicked. They were afraid the government was attacking them, so they barricaded themselves in offices.

"We're trying to bring about some meaningful change for the Indian community," an angry Dennis Banks told reporters that evening. "If this is the only action that will bring change, then you can count on demonstrations like this three hundred and sixty-five days a year."[1]

The next day, Banks and his groups of occupiers cleaned the offices and mopped and waxed the auditorium floor. They expected to move to better facilities that day, but the situation went from bad to worse. Over the next few days, the government threatened four times to empty the building. Each time, those inside prepared ways to defend themselves.

The occupation brought a lot of newspaper and television coverage. People around the country saw pictures on television of the BIA building where office furniture blocked entrances and covered windows. Newspapers ran photos of people holding weapons made out of table legs. Little was said, however, about the group leaders' efforts each day to get the Twenty Points before the government. Every evening, Banks and the others expected the guards to storm the building. Every morning, the government gave a new deadline for them to leave. The government had heard rumors that the occupied building was wired with explosives. This made the United States marshals unsure of what to do.

All of this was going on just five blocks from the White House. Spectators crowded the area. Some offered support in words or by giving food. Finally, White House aides met group leaders on the evening of November 6. The final order to leave the building was issued at that time. "If we receive no commitment [that the government will consider our demands] by midnight, then the Indian negotiators [will] have no alternative [but] to remove ourselves from the building and leave nothing," Banks told reporters. "There's been no business conducted in

— ◈ —

The Bureau of Indian Affairs (BIA) building that was the site of Native American occupation is shown here.

this building for years, and I'm sure there will be no business conducted here after the Indians leave."[2]

Negotiations concerning the Twenty Points went on for two days. Finally, the government agreed to respond. Those in the BIA building received permission to leave without being arrested. The government also gave them monetary assistance, since many of the churches and backers had withdrawn support. This government assistance drew sharp criticism from many sources, including conservative Native American organizations. They did not feel the government should pay to get back their building.

Some of the occupiers wrote things on the office walls and tore down maps and pictures. Some took official files and papers when they left the BIA building. Dennis Banks told reporters that the material contained "highly incriminating evidence." He felt the papers would prove government incompetence in its handling of Native American affairs.[3]

This vandalism and removal of government papers created outrage from the government and received a great deal of attention from the press. Many of the government papers were eventually returned. A few months later, as leader Hank Adams was negotiating to have more items returned, federal agents arrested him. At this time, Native Americans also learned that one of the people who traveled with them in the caravan was an FBI spy.

— ❖ —

Dennis Banks (center) helps an elderly demonstrator depart from the BIA building.

National feelings ranged from one extreme to another. "It's time for the government to get out of Indian Affairs entirely," said part of an editorial appearing in the *San Antonio Express/News.* The *Washington Evening Star* expressed the sentiments of many communities: ". . . the crowd that sacked the Bureau of Indian Affairs building obviously didn't represent a majority of Indians across the nation."[4]

Native Americans across the country also debated the effects of the BIA building occupation. Many older, government-connected organizations and leaders were upset by the vandalism. Yet in many parts of the country, sympathizers staged demonstrations of support.

In South Dakota, on the Pine Ridge Reservation, Richard (Dick) Wilson, the chairman of the Oglala Sioux Tribal Council, denounced the entire Trail of Broken Treaties Caravan. He was especially critical of AIM's involvement. Dick Wilson was a member of the Lakota tribe, but he was not a full-blood and did not follow traditional Lakota culture. He had been voted as tribal chairman in spring of 1972. Many at Pine Ridge had not participated in the election. Wilson also worked closely with white government officials. He was making plans to sell part of the Black Hills to the National Park Service, a deal that the tribal council had already rejected. The Black Hills are sacred to the Lakotas. Many older, full-blood members of the tribe claimed Wilson acted illegally.

Many young AIM leaders were from Pine Ridge. They had the support of the traditional Lakota elders, who wanted Wilson to step down from his position. As more people opposed him, Wilson fired several workers. He created a BIA tribal police force called Guardians of the Oglala Nation (GOON). Many of the locals began calling it the goon squad.

After the Trail of Broken Treaties, Wilson banned all AIM members from coming to the reservation to speak. He said, "If [AIM leader] Russell Means sets foot on this reservation, I, Dick Wilson, will personally cut off his braids."[5]

Wilson's ban on speakers to the reservation also included Dennis Banks. Banks, however, showed up at the reservation in late November to discuss the incident in Washington, D.C., with reservation people. A BIA policeman arrested him and escorted him off the reservation. Banks posted a small bond and was eventually released.

❖Government Reactions❖

Controversy continued about the Trail of Broken Treaties. Media opinions continued to be negative. Both AIM and the officials from the White House who had represented President Nixon were thought to have been in the wrong. The FBI listed AIM with such violent groups as the Simbianese Liberation Army, which robbed banks, and the Students for a Democratic Society (SDS), which blew up buildings. According to Dennis Banks, however, the occupation of the BIA building in Washington had been a spontaneous reaction to a bad situation.

The government cut off funding for the three AIM survival schools. Later, however, a federal judge released the funds for the good of the community. On December 27, 1972, after firing three top BIA officials, Secretary of Interior Roger Morton reported that he planned a complete reorganization of the BIA. Yet when the government finally responded to the Trail's

Twenty Points, they dismissed the plans as "wholly a backward step."[6]

◆Demonstrations Continue◆

Banks and other AIM leaders continued to promote their goals of community awareness and interaction between white and Native American communities. Upholding treaty rights was a continual issue. The Lincoln, Nebraska, chapter of AIM staged a nonviolent protest at Ft. Robinson, Nebraska, in November. This was the site of Crazy Horse's death in 1877. The activists protested the federal government's turnover of 316 acres of unused land to the state of Nebraska. AIM members claimed they could have followed treaty terms and allowed this land to automatically go back to the Oglala Nation. On November 20, Dennis Banks with John Two Bird Arbuckle and other protesters, traveled across Nebraska to Lincoln, the state capital, for a rally. They presented state officials with a list of demands and plans for the Fort Robinson land. They hoped to make it into an education and art center and to put a hospital there. They asked to speak with the governor, but the governor refused to meet with them.

◆Civil Rights Task Force◆

In mid-January of 1973, Dennis Banks and other AIM members visited Rapid City, South Dakota, to work with that city's Indian Civil Rights Task Force. In 1972, a serious summer flood of the Rapid River had devastated the city. It caused over two hundred deaths and millions of dollars in damage. The federal government was helping the city with money. Money promised to help rebuild the Native American community, however, never came. Mayor Donald

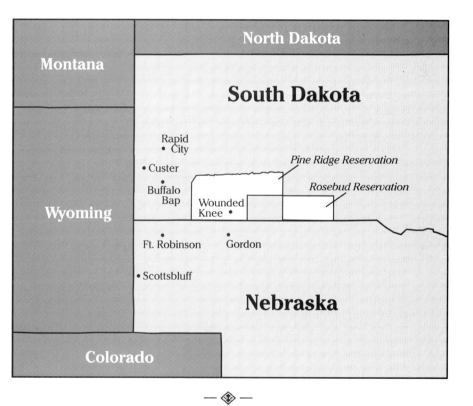

— ❖ —

The Pine Ridge Reservation and the Rosebud Reservation in South Dakota, sites of the turbulent events of 1972 to 1975, are shown on this map.

Barnett and the task force suspected possible racial discrimination, so they started an investigation.

While in Rapid City, Banks and AIM members were invited to the Chicano/Indio Unity Conference in Scottsbluff, Nebraska. The conference was hosted by The New Congress of Community Development (NCCD), a Chicano/Indio group. The mutual problems of the two groups would be discussed. Scottsbluff civil authorities responded angrily to the conference. Early one morning, they arrested several people, including AIM leader Russell Means. Means received injuries from a beating by police. When conference participants resumed their meeting at the NCCD office, the police kept officers outside. Leonard Crow Dog, a spiritual adviser to AIM, was also arrested. The organizing group finally made arrangements to have a hearing before a federal judge in Omaha. On January 24, a federal court ordered that law enforcement officials had to stop trying to bully the Native Americans.

During this time, just 120 miles away in Buffalo Gap, South Dakota, a white man had killed Wesley Bad Heart Bull, and Sarah Bad Heart Bull, was making contact with Dennis Banks and AIM leaders in Scottsbluff.

5

CHALLENGES

Custer, South Dakota, has a population of about twenty-one hundred people. It is forty-five miles from Rapid City, South Dakota, near Black Hills tourist areas such as Mount Rushmore and resort communities. This is where Banks had agreed to meet with state's attorney Hobart Gates about the Bad Heart Bull situation. Townspeople and state and local officials were uneasy about AIM's involvement.

State troopers and policemen in riot gear were on hand when Sarah Bad Heart Bull and many supporters arrived at the courthouse before the meeting. The only Native Americans allowed inside the building were Dennis Banks, Russell Means, Leonard Crow Dog, Dave Hill, and Robert High Eagle. High Eagle had been a witness to the crime. Everyone else stood outside in freezing temperatures and snow. After several hours, Sarah Bad Heart Bull attempted to go inside the building. She hoped to see how the negotiations were going, but police officers grabbed her. Her friends came to her aid, and a riot began.

By the time order was restored to the town, two police cars had been overturned and smoke and fire damaged part of the courthouse. Fire also burned the small wooden chamber of commerce building to the ground. Banks had been talking to the state's attorneys when the riot had started. A tear-gas canister was thrown into the room, and Banks was forced to leave by the window. Thirty people were arrested. Banks was questioned and released, but four days later he was charged with arson, burglary, and other crimes.

The Custer County Courthouse riot caused angry reactions throughout the region. The property destruction outraged whites. Native Americans felt the state and local police were to blame.

The next evening in Rapid City, local people and AIM leaders spent two hours talking with city leaders in a meeting arranged by Dennis Banks. Banks hoped to calm the racial tension. Mayor Donald Barnett promised to set up meetings with the mayors and police officials of nearby towns. Banks said, "These people [the local white governments] want us to live within their system, obey their laws, but they're not ready to lay down the law against their own kind."[1]

The meeting, meanwhile, did not produce positive results. White policemen from cities throughout the state took leaves of absence and went to Custer to help patrol the roads. National Guardsmen also arrived. The United States Attorney General sent sixty-five United States marshals to the Pine Ridge Reservation. Road blocks kept cars of Native Americans from getting to the area. The state governor sent troops to guard the armory building in the town of Pine Ridge.

Banks declared that as long as the militia was allowed "to go on the rampage in Custer and threaten every Indian's life with arms . . . then AIM will not consider anyone in Custer innocent."[2]

In Rapid City, more arrests occurred two days later, after racial violence resulted in more fighting. Forty Native Americans had been arrested, but no whites were. AIM members joined over one hundred other Native Americans who hurried to the jail. Riot police were in place around the jail. Banks and Russell Means persuaded those gathered to go home. Banks asked that all Native Americans abide by the newly-formed 9:30 P.M. curfew. AIM leaders and their attorney then met with officials to discuss the mass arrest.

❖Meetings About Civil Rights❖

On February 16, 1973, Dennis Banks addressed the senate of the state of South Dakota. It was the first such speech any Native American had presented to that body of government. Banks told of how he hoped for peaceful changes between communities. He said:

> I come here today to make a statewide appeal and to pledge to the citizens of South Dakota what we hope will become a move to further ease the tension, and . . . begin a new awareness of programs and ideas [for Native Americans] based on self-determination and self assistance.[3]

In Rapid City, representatives of the Civil Rights Working Commission and area churches met with Native Americans to discuss local problems. Other people argued, however, that Banks's statements were not valid. "I contend that if progress is to be made on racial conciliation, that AIM could have hired a representative for much less money than [was] spent for demonstrations and destruction . . .," said Dr. Larry Lytle of the Rapid City Common Council.[4]

Trouble with police continued, and on February 17, Dennis Banks and nine others filed a class-action suit in the United States District Court. A class action suit is a lawsuit where one or more people act to represent a whole group of people in a similar situation. This lawsuit was meant to stop officials from harassing Native Americans. Three days later, however, Judge Fred Nichol refused to order policemen to stop their actions toward Native Americans. On that same day, February 20, the Rapid City Council passed a resolution, part of which demanded that AIM "must refrain from assembly for any unlawful purpose, that AIM refrain from violence or threats of violence, and that AIM refrain from violating the laws."[5]

Banks replied, "It is ironic that an American Indian has to stand before this council and try to convince you we have a right to be here." He added, "I'd much rather you withdraw [the resolution] . . . lest open warfare break out in the city." One council member took this statement as a threat. A local physician noted that there had been threats of violence, but added, "You shouldn't have to do this to get your rights."[6]

Another Native American organization also expressed concerns about rights. The Oglala Sioux Civil Rights Organization (OSCRO) had started legal action to have tribal chairman, Dick Wilson removed from office. They scheduled a special hearing. Wilson canceled that hearing himself, even though hundreds of people had shown up. The hearing finally took place on February 22. Wilson would not answer questions and comments from those who were against him. People walked out. Many of the council members left. Although the council had twenty members, a 4-0 vote kept Dick Wilson in office.

The OSCRO people made a formal protest of Wilson's actions. They expressed concern about the modest amount of money the BIA charged outsiders for use of Oglala land. They also voiced their displeasure over the United States marshals who had been sent to the reservation after the Custer County Courthouse riot.

Dick Wilson banned meetings, but on February 27, 1973, more than five hundred reservation people attended a meeting held at Calico Hall, a community center. Dennis Banks was among them. United States marshals patrolled the area. The OSCRO members decided they needed to do something symbolic. They wanted the rest of the country to see what was going on at Pine Ridge, so the Oglala people turned to AIM.

At his 1974 trial, Dennis Banks said of the meeting:

> . . . in attendance at that meeting were Oglala Sioux chiefs, traditional headmen, medicine men, and councilmen. Eleven of the twenty councilmen were there . . . two women who were truly the real warriors of Indian society. . . asked where were the sprits of so long ago that made this nation [the Lakota Nation] great.
>
> They asked AIM what we were going to do about . . . the FBI and the marshals, allowing them to turn the village of Pine Ridge into an armed camp until . . . those people who were at Calico, were afraid to go to Pine Ridge. . . .

We'd reached a point in history where we could not tolerate that kind of abuse any longer, where these women, these parents, these mothers . . . could not see another Indian youngster die.[7]

❖Wounded Knee II❖

The symbolic action OSCRO decided on was to take place at the village of Wounded Knee. The tiny town consisted of a trading post, a church, and a few houses. There was also the mass grave of Lakota villagers killed by soldiers in 1890. That incident was referred to as Wounded Knee I. This was the same place where, five months earlier, Dennis Banks and Trail of Broken Treaties Caravan had stopped on their way to Washington, D.C.

Now Banks, Russell Means, tribal elders, and religious leaders led a caravan of several hundred people. Many of them were teenagers and women with their children. The United States marshals expected people might try to take over the BIA building in the town of Pine Ridge, but the cars and trucks moved on fifteen miles northeast of Pine Ridge Reservation, to Wounded Knee.

They took over the trading post, which was run by whites. It had, just the previous year, been raided and looted by a group of Native Americans. Most Lakota objected to the trading post which advertised with billboards like the following: "See the Wounded Knee Massacre Site, Visit the Mass Grave." This time, however, the activities, while illegal, were a bit more peaceful.

Dennis Banks warned people not to take anything from the store; however, weapons had already been taken from the trading post. Those who had weapons set up security around the area. They all expected the government forces to show up at any time. Most of the weapons were old hunting rifles. A few of the men who had fought in Vietnam had automatic weapons. The OSCRO leaders gathered the eleven people who lived in the main village and held them hostage.

Government officials had been watching them. They reacted immediately by closing off the four roads that led to Wounded Knee. Russell Means assumed a major role of AIM leadership, since he was Oglala. A phone call went out to authorities: "We hold the Knee," someone told them. They did not intend to give it up until the government either heard OSCRO's demands or killed them.[8] When government vehicles came too close, gunfire kept them away. The protesters wanted to talk only with Washington officials.

"What happens here at Wounded Knee has got to bring [help] to the Native American people all over this country," Banks wrote. His article was published in *Wassaja*, a national Native American newspaper out of San Francisco, California. "Here at Pine Ridge the conditions are miserable. We need housing, education, health care. And it's the same in too many places all over this country."[9]

David Long, vice president of the Pine Ridge Tribal Council, supported this view. "We don't have housing. There are no roads. There is no water. Three years ago I appeared before a [U.S.] Senate Committee requesting water. Congress appropriated money, but all they did was just drill holes."[10] Long told about the problems and the solutions he had attempted, including calls to the White House.

Inside the village, Dennis Banks again turned his efforts to the small community. He helped arrange care for the families. Many of them were unprepared for staying in Wounded Knee for more than a night. Community cooking was set up, and Banks became one of the camp leaders. He helped to coordinate the desires and responses of several tribal elders as well as other AIM members.

The government did not want any reporters in the area, but the national media went to Wounded Knee anyway. South Dakota senators George McGovern and newly elected James Abourezk visited the area the next day, March 1. They went through a series of FBI checkpoints set up along the road. The hostages told the senators that they did not intend to leave their property. The senators had several meetings with the Wounded Knee leadership. According to Senator Abourezk, the leaders agreed to give up the occupation if the FBI would inform the occupiers of their crimes so that they could begin a legal defense. Abourezk gave that information to the FBI before he returned to Washington, but the government forces never acted on it. The standoff continued.

Eventually, AIM leaders in Rapid City began talking with the government. The demands and responses of both sides often changed, but Banks maintained the position that high-level government officials must come to South Dakota to look into complaints of the Native Americans.

The government brought in more military equipment to surround the village. Around the nation, newspaper headlines and television news told of the standoff. Telegrams sent to the White House at first expressed anger about the hostages. Later, they became sympathetic to the Native American cause. In support of Wounded Knee II, the Crow tribe and the Northern Cheyenne tribe canceled mining leases on their reservations. The government called for a cease-fire on March 8. Very few people left the village, but nearly a hundred more people joined the forces inside. Many of them were not even Native American.

Many Wounded Knee legal residents did leave the area after the Sixth Army was called in, but some stayed. "Wounded Knee occupation people did not hold us by force," Wilbur Rieger later told reporters. "It was the military that was more responsible for holding us there. We were more the hostages of the military than [of] AIM."[11]

Nine families—about sixty people—stayed within the Native American defense lines during the entire occupation. The actions of the next two months displaced over two hundred residents of the town, nearby ranches, and farms.

In Wounded Knee, a hospital was set up in the only house that had electricity and running water. The museum became the security office. The store became the community center.

"You should listen to the bullets flying over our heads at night," Banks said.[12]

The new government blockade included seventeen armed personnel carriers. No one could pass through on the roads. Local people took back routes through the hills to smuggle food and medicine to Wounded Knee. The government sent up flares during the night so that they could spot those people who were trying to get to the village. The government used more flares in seventy-one days at Wounded Knee than they did during the entire Vietnam War.[13] A few private pilots flew in food supplies and dropped them down to the village. They had to be careful, however, to avoid government helicopters and fighter jets patrolling the area.

The elders proclaimed the community of Wounded Knee the Independent Oglala Nation. Banks became one of six elected councilmen, and spiritual leaders blessed the land. On Tuesday, March 13, Banks and other leaders had a meeting with local officials. A blizzard hit the area the next day. Roads were closed, with snowdrifts several feet high. The talks stalled until the weekend.

By this time, even international newspapers carried information about the dramatic situation. On March 26, the government again ordered all national news teams out of the area.

In April, a group of Oglalas negotiated some terms and received an invitation to Washington, D.C., to meet with government officials. A helicopter took Means, Crow Dog, and others out of Wounded Knee. For a while, many white residents of the area believed this marked the end of the siege, but this was not so. The meetings never came about, and the leaders returned to Wounded Knee, upset because no progress had been made.

April brought historic moments: Mary Brave Bird gave birth to a boy, whom she named Pedro. Little Pedro was the first birth in the newly formed Independent Oglala Nation. "He came into this world during the siege," his mother later wrote in her biography. "[W]ith bullets going through the wall and the drums beating before the window greeting the arrival of a new life. . . . A tiny victory in our people's struggle for survival."[14] A traditional Lakota marriage also took place.

The only two deaths of the occupation also occurred in April. On April 17, M-16 gunfire went through the walls of the church and killed Frank

— ◈ —

This cartoon showing President Richard Nixon with the "arrow" of Native American issues stuck to him illustrates the unchanging attitudes of many white people toward Native Americans in the 1970s.

Clearwater, who had arrived that day. Lakota Buddy Lamont, from the Pine Ridge Reservation, died from a wound after being struck by sniper fire on April 26. His family later buried him beside the historic Wounded Knee grave.

By the end of April, the occupiers were tense and distressed, and the government had other problems to worry about. The Watergate scandal of President Nixon's term had begun. Several high-level White House officials were forced from office. In Vietnam, United States forces were losing the battle for Saigon. Public opinion of the government was at an all-time low. Dennis Banks, and spiritual leader Leonard Crow Dog agreed it was time to end the situation. "We have accomplished what we came here to do," Banks told government negotiators, "so now we will quit."[15]

By the first week in May, agreements had been made. Banks and the others would put aside their weapons and surrender to authorities. The government promised a White House investigation of Oglala complaints. Later in the year, government hearings were held, but no decisions were made.

The surrender occurred on May 9, 1973. Dennis Banks had already left the camp. He spent several weeks visiting other reservations to learn the people's opinions. The FBI issued a federal arrest warrant for him. He surrendered on June 25, 1973, met the $105,000 bond, and was released until trial.

GOVERNMENT CONFLICTS

Dennis Banks's trial on the Wounded Knee charges was several months away, but he was still free to travel out of South Dakota. This allowed him to continue to promote AIM and the importance of treaty rights. At the ten-day AIM National Convention held in White Oak, Oklahoma, Banks was elected AIM National Director. The organization pledged itself to help change the government agencies that controlled native affairs. AIM also supported the activities of the United Farm Workers, led by activist Cesar Chavez.

✦Distrust Among AIM Members✦

Every time Banks traveled, the United States government seemed to know exactly where he was going. AIM leadership felt sure there was an informant for the federal authorities among them. Distrust became strong, even between people who had known each other for a long time.

In August, Banks traveled to Des Moines, Iowa, to meet with Governor Robert Ray. This meeting occurred after ten armed Native Americans took over a state office building in Des Moines in an action that had been started by Douglass Durham. Durham had become an active AIM member during Wounded Knee II.

What happened in Des Moines was not an official AIM action. The event ended without violence, and all involved were arrested. The meeting between Banks and Governor Ray produced plans for Native American problems to be discussed by city officials.

Later in August, a South Dakota court dismissed riot and assault charges on twenty-two of the Custer County Courthouse defendants. Charges against Dennis Banks were not dropped, however. In September, the court charged him with starting the riot and with assault. Anti-AIM attitudes were on the rise, especially in South Dakota. Banks decided he would not get a fair hearing, so he did not appear in the South Dakota court for it. He and a few others disappeared.

The FBI put out a federal fugitive arrest warrant on him, but Banks had left the country. He traveled to the north of Canada near the Arctic Circle, and he stayed there until the money for his bond had been raised. That way he would not have to spend very much time in jail.

Douglass Durham helped Banks return to Rapid City. He even flew the rented plane that got Banks back. The Wounded Knee trials began January 8, 1974. By then, Durham was Banks's assistant and coordinator of the Wounded Knee Legal Defense/Offense Committee (WKLDOC). He had scheduled many of Dennis Banks's public appearances and set up news conferences.

Nearly a year later, AIM discovered that Douglass Durham was a professional undercover agent. He had been working as an FBI informant ever since he had shown up at Wounded Knee. His assignment was to get close to the top leadership of AIM.

The Wounded Knee trial took place in St. Paul, Minnesota. In opening statements Banks said: "Wounded Knee represented the last pint, the last blood transfusion. It was unfortunate that . . . Indians have died, but they died knowing . . . that the unborn generations will be given that opportunity to live the life that they choose, and not the life that somebody else dictates."[1]

— ❖ —

Dennis Banks is shown here in Hobridge, South Dakota, in 1974.

❖The Wounded Knee Trial❖

The trial took eight months. The prosecution used six of those months to present its case about the eleven counts against Banks and Russell Means. Because of evidence given by the defense team, however, the prosecution could not use a great deal of its information. In July, Judge Fred Nichol dismissed five of the eleven charges. He said the prosecution had not presented enough evidence to prove them. The other counts were scheduled to go before a jury.

The AIM defense teams remained very busy. Other Wounded Knee trials were going on in three states. The Custer County Courthouse trials were also taking place in Rapid City. There, on June 20, 1974, presiding judge Joseph Bottum sentenced three people, including Sarah Bad Heart Bull, to the state prison. The court allowed her only twenty-four hours to make arrangements for her four young children before sending her to prison. National Native American organizations, including AIM and Dennis Banks, started a Free Sarah Bad Heart Bull campaign, and her sentence was eventually reduced from five years to five months. Darold Schmidt, who was accused of killing her oldest son, Wesley, was acquitted and never served any jail time.

The prosecutor at the Custer County Courthouse trial was William Janklow. He had at one time been a legal-aid attorney on the Rosebud Reservation. He was running in the fall election to become the state attorney general. Janklow called the verdict against Sarah Bad Heart Bull and the others a "victory for the people of South Dakota."[2]

Later that autumn, Dennis Banks and lawyers petitioned the Rosebud Reservation Tribal Court to disbar William Janklow because of something that had happened years before. The tribal court did ban him from practicing law on the reservation, but in November, South Dakota voters elected Janklow to the post of attorney general. In years to come, William Janklow would have a great impact on Dennis Banks's life.

In St. Paul, while the Banks-Means Wounded Knee trial was in recess, Banks traveled to Kenora, Canada, where armed Anishinabe had taken over a park. Banks made good use of his skills as a negotiator, and the situation ended without violence.

Soon after that, on September 13, there was good news in Minnesota. The jury voted 12-0 to acquit Banks and Means. All charges were dropped. AIM members and supporters held a victory party.

In his closing remarks, Judge Nichol said:

> In deciding this motion, I have taken into consideration the prosecution's conduct throughout the entire trial. The fact that incidents of misconduct formed a pattern . . . leads me to the belief that this case was not prosecuted in good faith or in the spirit of justice.[3]

The United States Justice Department disagreed with the results. But the acquittal and dismissal of charges stood.

— ❖ —

Dennis Banks (third from left) is shown here with Russel Means (second from left) in St. Paul, Minnesota, with their counsel William Kuntsler (left) and Mark Lane (right).

Throughout 1974 and early 1975, Dennis Banks continued to give speeches and attend rallies in support of AIM. All of the fees he received went directly to AIM.

In March of 1975, AIM leaders had gathered proof that Douglass Durham was a spy. Durham, however, said he had a deep respect for Dennis Banks. "I wish I were half the man that Dennis is," Durham told *Christian Century* correspondent John Adams. "He is a viable, logical and peaceful leader of a necessary social protest movement."[4]

— ◈ —

In St. Paul, Minnesota, Russel Means (left seated), Dennis Banks (right seated, with vest), and supporters celebrate the dismissal of the Wounded Knee charges.

The United States Senate planned a special June hearing to look into the matter. However, this did not lessen the anti-AIM attitude in South Dakota. On the Pine Ridge Reservation, Dick Wilson defeated Russell Means in an election for tribal chairman. The voting procedures were questioned, but the Justice Department took no action. Wilson ordered all those who had voted for Means off the reservation. He and GOON stepped up his war against AIM members and Oglala traditionals.

"The real victims of law and order on this reservation are the full-blood Indians," said Al Trimble, an Oglala who was a BIA superintendent in the area.

> [H]alf of our BIA cops were Wilson people . . . And those white cowboys in the area were boasting about all their guns and about how they were going to shoot those 'longhairs' first and let the court ask questions later because they knew they could get away with it in South Dakota.[5]

Beatings occurred and firebombs damaged houses. Information and complaints sent to federal authorities, including the FBI, were ignored. "It is clear that the FBI has conducted their activities on the Pine Ridge Reservation in such a manner as to leave the Bureau with little or no credibility . . .," wrote South Dakota senator James Abourezk to the United States Attorney General.[6]

During early 1975, Dennis Banks and his Oglala wife, Darlene "Kamook" Nichols, lived on the Rosebud Reservation in a log cabin. They had a baby daughter, and Kamook was expecting another child. In May, Banks and his family left the state for a series of meetings and the national AIM convention in Farmington, New Mexico. Russell Means did not attend these meetings. On June 8, in South Dakota, a BIA policeman shot him in the back. Means was wounded, but not fatally. This same month Banks was to return to Rapid City for the Custer County Courthouse riot charges. At this time, the FBI sent forty more armed agents in and around the Pine Ridge Reservation.

On June 26, Banks returned to Rapid City to face charges for his part in the Custer County Courthouse riot. Many people were at the courthouse. William Janklow, the state attorney general, had traveled two hundred miles from the capital to lead the case against Banks. "[H]e even accosted me in the hallway," Banks reported, "and said he was going to get me."[7]

❖Banks Convicted on Custer Riot Charges❖

A month later, on July 26, the judge convicted Dennis Banks on the Custer County Courthouse riot charges. A hearing was set to determine how much time Banks would have to spend in jail. Banks was released on bond and continued to be optimistic. At a speech soon after in Nebraska, he repeated the goals he had lived for and taught since 1968. "We [AIM members] are rekindling the dream. We want recognition of our sovereignty, the rebuilding of our nation's hope. We need to reclaim our spirituality. We need the government to end this longest war."[8]

The annual Sun Dance was held at Rosebud from August 1 to 4. On August 5, the court expected Dennis Banks to appear for sentencing, but he did not. Again, the FBI issued a fugitive warrant for Dennis Banks's arrest. He would be a federal fugitive for many years to come.

UNCERTAINTIES

"The 'First People' such as myself are born running for a better way of life, and an even chance. . . . Indian people are in virtual exile in their own homeland."[1]   —Dennis Banks

Along with South Dakota authorities, officials in Oregon also had a warrant for Banks's arrest. They believed he had been the driver of a motor home in which explosives and firearms were found. Kamook Banks and her baby daughter were passengers in the motor home. The Oregon State Highway Patrol arrested them. They also arrested Russell Redner, Kenneth Loudhawk, and Anna Mae Aquash. The motor home driver, believed to be Banks, and another person, believed to be activist Leonard Peltier, got away.

The FBI caught up with Dennis Banks in the San Francisco suburb of El Cerrito, California, in January 1976. In the time between August 1975 and January 1976, Banks had not been in hiding. In fact, he had traveled through the United States and Canada, visiting reservations and meeting with tribal chairmen and traditional people. He had even attended classes at Contra Costa Community College in California.

In the early morning of the January 24, 1976, more than thirty armed agents surrounded the California home of Lehman Brightman where Banks was staying. Brightman was a Lakota professor of Native American studies at Contra Costa Community College. He had founded the United Native Americans organization in 1968, and was a longtime friend of Banks. When the agents arrested Banks, he said, "I was born an Indian, and even [with] the threat of spending my entire life in jail in chains, I will not submit my ways and beliefs to be somebody else; I am proud of being an Indian. I will die within that pride."[2]

❖Banks Seeks Sanctuary in California❖

Banks appealed to California's governor, Edmund G. (Jerry) Brown, to let him stay in California. Banks felt that going back to South Dakota could mean his death. A documented report was presented at a later trial. In it, one white man who lived on the Rosebud

— ❖ —

Dennis Banks always stood behind his belief in the importance of stressing rights for all Native Americans.

Reservation declared, "Dennis Banks is a marked man in South Dakota. . . . There must be over one thousand white men in South Dakota who would consider themselves heroes if they shot Dennis Banks."[3]

In the three years that followed Wounded Knee II, there were sixty-three unsolved murders of Native Americans on the Pine Ridge Reservation. The FBI Uniform Crime Reports for 1975 reported that the murder rate at Pine Ridge was eighteen times higher than the national average.[4]

Before Banks posted bail, thousands of people attended a rally in San Francisco, California, to support Dennis Banks. Church organizations urged the California attorney general to examine the attitudes in South Dakota. Governor Brown received a petition with 150,000 signatures, asking him not to return Banks to South Dakota.

There was a hearing about Banks being sent to Oregon, and the courtroom overflowed with supporters. On February 9, Banks told the crowded courtroom, "I only hope the people here will be able to read the real story of what's going on on Indian reservations across the country."[5] He returned to Brightman's home in El Cerrito.

The California governor's legal director offered to jail Banks for up to fifteen years, and Banks agreed to this. Banks was willing to serve his jail time in any state other than South Dakota. However, this did not satisfy South Dakota's attorney general William

Janklow, so Janklow took the issue to the California Supreme Court.

Later that month, Anna Mae Aquash was found dead on the Pine Ridge Reservation. Prior to her death, she had been missing for four months. After Aquash had been arrested with Kamook Banks and her infant daughter by Oregon highway patrol, she had returned to Pierre, South Dakota, in November to face questioning about the murders of two FBI agents from the previous summer. Several friends and family members said she was afraid that she would be killed. Her body was not found until February. After the identification of her body, an FBI spokesman said that "some members of AIM might have suspected that Miss Aquash was a government informer."[6]

To clear up any such suspicion, Banks and other AIM leaders organized their own internal investigation. They found that no AIM member was involved. In a public statement Banks said, "Annie Mae Aquash was a dear friend and a trusted friend. . . . Her murder is another example of an FBI cover-up in the attempt to destroy the leadership of the American Indian Movement."[7] Anna Mae Aquash's murder was never solved.

❖Banks Goes to Oregon❖

In April 1976, Banks traveled to Portland, Oregon, to face the firearms charges. Hundreds of supporters greeted him with banners, flags, and music. William

Janklow appealed to Oregon's governor Robert Straub to send Banks back to South Dakota after the Oregon trial. Native Americans from many states traveled to Portland to give Banks their support. Groups began their efforts to keep Governor Straub from sending Banks back. Banks had backing from some well-known people. Among them were basketball star Bill Walton, comedian Dick Gregory, and attorney William Kuntsler. Entertainers Tony Bennett and Harry Belafonte offered to perform benefit concerts.

While Banks awaited the trial, support for him grew. The state American Civil Liberties Union (ACLU) wrote to Governor Straub: "The ACLU of Oregon urges you to deny South Dakota's request to extradite Dennis Banks because we believe his life would be in danger if he were returned."[8] A North Dakota state senator traveled to Oregon to tell the court of the injustices to native people in the Dakotas.

Jerry Running Foxe of the Coquille was a candidate for Oregon's Fourth Congressional District. He and his people sponsored a special meeting at which Banks, codefendant Russell Redner, and other supporters spoke. After the meeting, Banks joined Running Foxe and others at a local hospital, where they held a prayer service for two Native Americans who were unable to attend the meeting.

❖Charges Dropped❖

The trial on May 12 was very short. Judge Robert Belloni dismissed the firearms and explosive charges against the defendants. The main reason for the dismissal was because the prosecution said they were not ready. The dismissal was *with prejudice*, meaning that if the prosecution got evidence of new charges, they could take the defendants to court again. Several years later, they did just that. Governor Straub also chose not to send Banks back to South Dakota, so Banks returned to California.

❖Banks in California❖

Banks and his family lived in Davis, California, where Banks completed classes he had been taking at nearby D-Q University. D-Q University is a private, two-year college created in 1971 to serve Native American and Chicano students. It is the only accredited intertribal Native American college in California.

Banks also stayed busy teaching classes at the university. Meanwhile, the California Supreme Court debated on whether or not to send him back to South Dakota. The court finally decided that it was up to Governor Brown, and Banks remained in California.

Most other key AIM leaders were either in jail or awaiting trial on various Wounded Knee-related charges. Clyde Bellecourt continued the survival schools and housing programs in Minnesota. Other chapters worked independently, just as Banks did in California, to continue the overall goals of AIM.

❖The Longest Walk❖

In 1978, Banks organized a nationwide demonstration called the Longest Walk. He was protesting anti-Indian Senate bills that would totally do away with historic treaties. The protest began in March in California, and was supported by church organizations, social groups, and even heavyweight boxing champion Ken Norton. Banks could start the walk, but he could not leave California without being arrested. The protest was a success. The June

— ❖ —

Dennis Banks worked throughout the 1970s to continue the overall goals of AIM.

statement from the Washington office of the Longest Walk stated its two-fold purpose as follows:

1) to educate the American/World community about our struggle, and 2) to bring about public attention on eleven anti-Indian bills now before Congress. If enacted, these bills would take away the rights of Indian people to control their lives, their children, and their communities.[9]

Thousands of Native Americans arrived in Washington, D.C., in mid-July. These protesters obtained permission to camp in a section of a nearby Virginia park. The government supplied showers and security, and sweat lodges were set up. Spiritual leaders led ceremonies. The Longest Walk and the public awareness it created stopped the bills the Native Americans were protesting from becoming law.

Autumn of 1978 saw a change in South Dakota. Voters elected William Janklow as governor. Janklow vowed once again to get Banks out of California. For the next few years, however, this was not possible.

❖Banks Stays Active❖

As chancellor of D-Q University, Banks was in charge of funds and culture. He was also a visiting professor at Stanford University. He lectured on federal Indian law and taught Indian studies. He spoke out constantly against child abuse and the abuse of alcohol and drugs. He established rescue missions of food and clothing for the needy. He also continued to raise money for the legal cases that continued against AIM members.

One of those legal cases was that of Leonard Peltier. Peltier and three other men were accused of shooting the FBI agents at Rosebud in 1975. Weak evidence allowed for the release of one man. The other two were freed because they had acted in self defense. Yet in 1977, Peltier received a sentence of life imprisonment for the killings. "Free Leonard" protests have taken place around the world.[10]

In January of 1982, the other leaders of AIM went to California. It was the first time in a number of years they had all met, and they made plans for AIM to become more active.

> We discussed what is happening to Indian people in El Salvador and Guatemala . . . and what we could do for [our people who are in prison]. And finally we asked Clyde Bellecourt to put the national office in Minneapolis back together: the American Indian Movement is alive again![10]

Yet later that year, the situation did not look good for Banks. In an upset election victory, George Deukmejian replaced Jerry Brown as governor of California. Deukmejian had already stated that if elected, he would not continue to help Banks. Banks's supporters made several attempts to change Deukmejian's mind, but they could not.

Deukmejian was sworn in on January 3, 1983. That afternoon, federal marshals went after Banks.

They had a warrant for his arrest that would send him back to South Dakota. There, he would serve time for the Custer County Courthouse Riot.

When the federal marshals arrived at Banks's house, Banks was not there. He had already left California and fled to safety with the Onondaga people in New York State, where he had many friends. Oren Lyons, one of the tribal chiefs, had brought several Onondaga people to Wounded Knee in 1973.

❖Life Among the Onondagas❖

Onondagas are part of the Iroquois Confederacy, also known as the League of Six Nations. They feel very strongly about treaty rights. The 1784 Treaty of Fort Stanwix assured independence for the Iroquois. To this day, they are not under control of the United States government. Tribal members are Iroquois citizens and travel on Iroquois passports. The city of Syracuse is built on Onondaga land, which New York State leases from the tribe.

For a few months, Banks's situation was uncertain. He and his family were living on the 7,300-acre reservation, but just temporarily. Rumor suggested he had been offered refuge in Cuba. It was also said that actor Marlon Brando had agreed to let Banks stay on his South Seas island. Banks said, "Even though I am hounded from one end of this country to the other, I will never abandon it completely."[11]

The fifteen chiefs of the Iroquois Nation called a special meeting, and in March 1983 they allowed Banks official sanctuary as protection. This was fortunate for Banks, because the newly elected governor of New York State, Mario Cuomo, did not pledge to protect Banks as Jerry Brown had done in California. Banks had to stay on the Onondaga reservation. There was some worry that the FBI might raid the reservation to arrest him, but that never happened.

Banks also had to consider a return to Oregon. There, he would answer new charges on the weapons violations from the motor home incident. On May 2, 1983, however, a federal judge dismissed those charges. The next year, the United States Court of Appeals upheld the decision to dismiss charges. But the Oregon case would keep popping up in Banks's life.

Banks remained involved while in the Onondaga community. He was always ready to aid the welfare of others. He organized food and clothing drives for reservations in South Dakota during the frigid winter of 1983. He also coached the reservation's cross-country running club. He personally ran six miles a day. He began building a house for Kamook and their children. A newspaper in Syracuse even invited him to write a weekly column.

❖The Longest Run❖

In 1984, the United States hosted the Olympic Games in Los Angeles, California. That year, Banks became the principal organizer of the Great Jim Thorpe Longest Run, an eight-week nationwide cross-country relay with Native American runners. Banks ran the first three miles with the Onondagas. He stopped at the edge of the reservation, since he could not leave. The other runners carried medicine bundles from the Onondaga reservation in New York. They ran across fourteen states to arrive in Los Angeles at the time of the Olympics. There, the Native American Fine Arts Society sponsored a Jim Thorpe Memorial Powwow to honor Thorpe's winning of the decathlon and pentathlon medals in the 1912 Olympics.

❖Banks Faces Sentencing in Custer❖

In September 1984, Banks decided to end his exile. He returned to South Dakota to face sentencing on the 1973 Custer County Courthouse charges. He was brought to court in handcuffs and leg irons on October 8. The courtroom overflowed with specta-tors. Many witnesses testified to Banks's good character. They told of how he had helped people on Pine Ridge. People also came from California to speak on his behalf. They told of the positive changes he had made in the lives of many people. With so many witnesses, the sentencing took all day.

Before his sentence was announced, Banks made a statement to the court. He told about his former jail time when he discovered what he should be doing with his life. He spoke of the events that led to the Custer Courthouse riot.

> *I am prepared to do whatever time you give me. I'm prepared also to help build South Dakota. . . . I came back [to South Dakota] because progress is too slow. Progress in trying to bring together Indian people and white people is too slow.*[12]

The judge sentenced Banks to three years, the longest prison term given to any of the people convicted for the Custer County Courthouse riot.

STILL ACTIVE

The Custer County Courthouse riot of 1973 finally had closure. The governor of Wisconsin offered to exchange Banks for another prisoner. This way Banks could serve his time in Wisconsin, but Banks refused. "I felt that if there was still racism in the prison system, that I wanted to meet it head on, and not run from it. So I declined the invitation." The publicity about Banks's return and sentencing set a tone in the prison. "They [the guards] said they were going to treat me just like any other prisoner, and they did."[1]

Banks served fourteen months in the South Dakota prison before being paroled. He later moved back to the Pine Ridge Reservation with employment as a part-time alcoholism counselor. For the first six months, he could not leave the state, but after that, with approval from his parole officer, he could travel throughout the country.

The counselor position Banks took was at Loneman School in the town of Oglala, twenty miles from Wounded Knee. The school is a former federal day-school, built by the BIA. In 1975, President Gerald Ford, who succeeded Nixon after the Watergate scandal, signed into law the Indian Education Assistance Act. This allowed interested Native Americans to start and run their own federal programs. Under this new government system, the Oglala community took over operation of the school.

Even with this change, Pine Ridge had not shown much change since the early 1970s. Employment had not improved, and housing remained substandard: Many families still lived in old trailers or patched and poorly insulated houses. The towns had few stores, and there were no theaters or other places of entertainment. Alcoholism affected many families.

❖Banks Does Community Work❖

Working on a local level seemed to suit Banks. He began a personal campaign to attract business and industry to the reservation. In 1986, Banks reported,

*We have timber. We started a brand-new saw mill
and got it rolling. . . . Another project is cabling and
harnessing for Honeywell. . . . Then there's quilting.
We have about fifty to sixty backorders for the
blankets we make here.*[2]

Banks no longer challenged government
authority. The projects he promoted were different
from his previous tactics of the early 1970s, but they
still represented the concerns of AIM. "I'm working
here at Loneman Industries, and everything that I do
reflects on what I believe in AIM orientation. . . .
[P]utting all these people to work here? For me that's
leadership."[3]

During his parole, Banks also hosted a radio show
on the local Oglala-run station, KILI. The weekly program featured local culture and country-western
music by popular Native American and white singers.
Banks used the program to continue spreading his
messages about the negative effects of drug abuse
and alcoholism.

❖Decades of Change❖

In the years since Dennis Banks helped to start AIM in
Minneapolis, Minnesota, many changes had taken
place in the country. "The awareness created by
AIM," Banks said, ". . . had a great impact on the
white public out there. . . . I don't know how we can
measure the impact of AIM, but I do know that there
have been major changes in this country on policies
affecting our people. Some have been positive."[4]

The government made several important policy shifts. In December 1970, President Nixon signed a law that restored the sacred Blue Lake to the people of Taos, New Mexico. In 1972, Mt. Adams, Washington, sacred land of the Yakimas, was restored to them. In 1974, following the events on the Pine Ridge Reservation, the United States District Court in the state of Washington made a landmark decision, upholding the fishing rights of Native Americans in Washington.

Other Native American organizations continued to be very active. The Native American Rights Fund was organized in 1971. This group won many court battles and influenced Congress on the protection of tribal natural resources, human rights, and the preservation of tribal existence.

In the years since Dennis Banks went underground to avoid sentencing, AIM shifted its energies back to regional social concerns. One of those issues was the destruction of Native American graves and human remains. There were often lectures and public awareness meetings about this problem. In the states of Indiana and Kentucky, Banks joined with Native American organizations to influence lawmakers. Those states passed laws to protect grave sites. Banks later participated in the Uniontown, Kentucky, ceremonies for reburial of more than twelve hundred grave sites that had been violated by grave robbers.

❖Back in Court❖

This positive influence on lawmakers did not halt the one legal battle that Banks still had to face. The Oregon firearms charges from 1974 still stood. The district and federal courts had dismissed the case on legal technicalities, but the attorney for the prosecution filed a fourth appeal in the fall of 1986. All through 1987 Banks's attorneys argued in court and filed papers. Finally, on March 8, 1988, Banks pleaded guilty to illegal possession of dynamite, and was sentenced to five years—all on probation.

— ❖ —

Native American elders particpate in part of the four-year ceremonies for reburial of bones.

Through all of this, Banks remained fit and active. He participated in the Sacred Run Foundation, an organization he started in the 1980s. The concept that was effective in the Jim Thorpe ceremony of 1984 continues to be a way to promote peace and understanding between all peoples. "The message that the Sacred Run puts forth is that all life is Sacred, and that we as human beings have duties and responsibilities to this planet that we call Mother Earth."[5] Banks developed an international run in 1988 that started in New York and extended to Japan.

❖Wounded Knee II Anniversary❖

February 1993 marked the twentieth anniversary of Wounded Knee II. Banks returned to South Dakota and joined other people who had been involved at Wounded Knee. They met at the historic grave site on the Pine Ridge Reservation. Here Buddy Lamont, the Oglala victim of 1973, lay buried alongside the mass grave of the Oglala who were killed 103 years earlier. Extreme violence on the reservation had continued from 1973 through the spring of 1976. In the 1990s, however, industry and harmony had begun among former adversaries. Banks and most others had put aside the bad feelings from the 1970s.

❖A Man of Many Hats❖

Banks has never put aside his quest for legal rights for Native Americans. He organized and led the 1994

Walk for Justice, a project that began in California and ended in Washington, D.C. Banks hoped to bring national awareness to the grievances of Native Americans. The walk also served as a means to collect signatures of many concerned people who urged the release of Leonard Peltier.

Banks also participated in Hollywood movies. The film industry has changed over the years, and Native Americans are now cast to portray Native Americans roles. The movie *Thunderheart* (1992) presents a fictional story in a setting quite similar to events that happened in South Dakota in the 1970s. Banks portrays a member of the fictional radical group A.R.M. He also has roles in *War Party* (1989) and *The Last of the Mohicans* (1993).

Banks's life has been chronicled in *Current Biography Yearbook* (1992), *Contemporary Newsmakers*, and *Native America: Portrait of the Peoples*, for which Banks wrote the foreword. His autobiography entitled *Sacred Soul* was published in Japan. The book won that country's National Book Award.

In 1997, Banks agreed to lead the "Bring Peltier Home" campaign that included teach-ins, concerts, and petition drives. AIM chapters and Peltier-support groups from around the world came together to talk about how they could assist in the release of Peltier. A Run for Freedom was also held in June 1997. It went from Cincinnati, Ohio, to Tulsa, Oklahoma, and was sponsored by the Sacred Run Foundation.

Banks has used his Sacred Run Foundation to spread warnings about the use of alcohol and drugs. He promotes Native American spirituality as a way to overcome these problems. "Alcohol was never a part of our rituals and ceremonies. It was never part of our lives at all until two hundred and three hundred years ago," he often says. The foundation hosts Sobriety Powwows in which Native Americans from several different tribes participate.

At a Sobriety Powwow held at Northern Kentucky University, Banks said, "For Indians, celebrating the passage of time in a sober way is the traditional way; it's the original way."[6]

The traditional way has been a guiding force in Banks's life and actions since 1968. He has always been willing to negotiate and plan for a calmer, more productive future. In this country and on other continents, Banks gives lectures and leads workshops on spiritual living. He continues to support Native American sovereignty as he travels from one side of this country to the other in his quest to increase national awareness about Native American rights and cultures.

Ꭸ CHRONOLOGY Ꭸ

1932 ❖ Dennis Banks is born on Leech Lake Reservation in Minnesota.

1937 −1951 ❖ Attends government boarding schools.

1953 ❖ Enlists in the Air Force.

1958 ❖ Is discharged and returns to Minnesota.

1966 ❖ Is imprisoned at Stillwater, Minnesota.

1968 ❖ Is paroled. Founds the American Indian Movement (AIM) with Clyde Bellecourt, George Mitchell, and Pat Ballenger.

1969 ❖ Occupies Alcatraz Island, California. Occupation lasts nineteen months.

1972 ❖ Leads Trail of Broken Treaties caravan to Washington, D.C.

November 2: Leads takeover of BIA Headquarters in Washington, D.C.

1973 ❖ **February 6:** Leads Custer County Courthouse Riot, Custer, South Dakota.

February 27-May 9: Leads takeover and government siege of Wounded Knee Village.

1974 ❖ **June:** Participates in First International Treaty Conference in Hobredge, South Dakota.

September: Wounded Knee charges are dismissed.

1975 ❖ **July 26:** Is convicted on Custer County Courthouse riot charges.

August 5: Becomes a federal fugitive through September 1984.

1976 ❖ Graduates from Contra Costa Community College in San Pablo, California. Is made a Chancellor at D-Q University, California.

1978 ❖ Organizes the Longest Walk.

1983 ❖ Moves to Onondaga Reservation to avoid prosecution.

1984 ❖ **March:** Organizes Jim Thorpe Run.

September: Surrenders to South Dakota authorities.

October 8: Is sentenced to three years in prison for the Custer County Courthouse riot.

1986 ❖ **January:** Is paroled. Becomes an alcoholism counselor on Pine Ridge Reservation.

March 8: Pleads guilty to illegal possession of dynamite. Is sentenced to five years on probation.

1988 ❖ Organizes Sacred Run Foundation International Run in the United States and Japan. His autobiography is published in Japan.

1994 ❖ Organizes the Walk for Justice.

1997 ❖ Continues as director of Sacred Run Foundation and field director of AIM. Continues in his role as a noted speaker, and in the "Free Leonard Peltier" effort.

CHAPTER NOTES

Chapter 1
1. United States Bureau of the Census, Government Printing Office, Washington, D.C., 1970.

Chapter 2
1. Arlene Hirschfelder and Martha Kreipe de Montaño, *The Native American Almanac: A Portrait of Native America Today* (New York: Prentice Hall General Reference and Travel, 1993), p. 40.

2. Ibid., p. 279.

3. "Dennis Banks Arrested," *Akwesasne Notes*, Mohawk Nation, Vol. 8, No. 1, 1976, p. 15.

4. Ibid.

5. Kenneth Stern, *Loudhawk: The United States Versus the American Indian Movement* (Norman, Okla.: University of Oklahoma Press, 1994), p. 249.

6. "Dennis Banks Arrested," p. 15.

7. Ibid.

Chapter 3
1. Mary Crow Dog with Richard Erdoes, *Lakota Woman* (New York: Grove Press, 1990), p. 76.

2. Vine Deloria, Jr., *We Talk, You Listen* (New York: MacMillan, 1970), p. 114.

3. Ibid., p. 100.

4. American Indians Unlimited, *Declaration of Purpose* (Ann Arbor, Mich.: American Indians Unlimited, 1969), unpaged.

5. Carl Waldham with Molly Braun, *Atlas of the North American Indian* (New York: Facts on File, 1985), p. 201.

6. Helen L. Peterson, "Who Speaks for the Native American?" *The Journal of Intergroup Relations* (New York: National Association of Human Rights Workers, Vol. III, No. 3, Summer 1974), p. 37.

7. Joseph Lelyveld, "Indians' Bid to Seize Ellis Island Foiled," *The New York Times*, March 17, 1970, p. 45.

8. National Indian Youth Council, *News Release*, Albuquerque, New Mexico, March 26, 1970, p. 6.

9. Jim Shaefer (UPI), "History Play Interrupted by Indians," *The Holland Michigan Evening Sentinel*, July 27, 1970, p. 6.

10. Ibid.

11. Robert Hagen, "Minnesota Indians Occupy Naval Station," *Minneapolis Tribune*, May 22, 1971, p. 27.

12. Arlene Hirschfelder and Martha Kreipe de Montaño, *The Native American Almanac: A Portrait of Native America Today* (New York: Prentice Hall General Reference and Travel, 1993) pp. 41, 284.

13. Kenneth Stern, *Loudhawk: The United States Versus the American Indian Movement* (Norman, Okla.: University of Oklahoma Press, 1994), p. 326.

14. Akwesasne Notes, *Trail of Broken Treaties: B.I.A. I'm Not Your Indian Any More* (Mohawk Nation, 1974), p. 3.

Chapter 4

1. Akwesasne Notes, *Trail of Broken Treaties: B.I.A. I'm Not Your Indian Any More* (Mohawk Nation, 1974), p. 11.

2. Ibid., p. 19.

3. Ibid., p. 26.

4. Ibid., p. 48.

5. Ibid., p. 34.

6. Peter Matthiessen, *In the Spirit of Crazy Horse* (New York: Viking, 1991), p. 56.

Chapter 5

1. "Showdown at Custer," *Akwesasne Notes*, Vol. 5, No. 2, 1973, p. 6.
2. Ibid., p. 7.
3. "Trouble at Rapid City," *Akwesasne Notes*, Vol. 5, No. 2, 1973, p. 10.
4. Ibid.
5. Ibid.
6. Ibid.
7. *U.S.* vs. *Dennis Banks & Russell Means*, U.S. District Court, St. Paul, Minn., February 12, 1974.
8. Mary Crow Dog with Richard Erdoes, *Lakota Woman* (New York: Grove Press, 1990), p. 127.
9. Dennis Banks, "We Were Asked to Come to Wounded Knee," *Wassaja*, February/March 1973, p. 4.
10. Ibid.; David Long, "Sioux Tribe Leader Speaks Out."
11. "Hostages Ask Marshals to Leave Area," *Wassaja*, February-March 1973, p. 4.
12. "We Were Asked To Come to Wounded Knee," p. 4.
13. Kenneth Stern, *Loudhawk: The United States Versus the American Indian Movement* (Norman, Okla.: University of Oklahoma Press, 1994), p. 336.
14. Mary Brave Bird with Richard Erdoes, *Ohitika Woman* (New York: Grove Press, 1993), p. 54.
15. Stanley D. Lyman, *Wounded Knee 1973: A Personal Account* (Lincoln, Neb.: University of Nebraska Press, 1991), p. 133.

Chapter 6

1. Rex Weyler, *Blood of the Land: The Government and Corporate War Against the American Indian Movement* (New York: Everest House, 1982), p. 113.
2. "Custer Trial Goes On" *Akewsasne Notes*, Vol. 6, No. 3, 1974, p. 16.
3. Martin Waldron, "2 Freed as Judge Scores U.S. Wounded Knee Case," *The New York Times*, September 17, 1974, p. 1.

4. John P. Adams, "AIM, the Church and the FBI: The Douglass Durham Case," *The Christian Century*, May 14, 1975, p. 493.

5. Peter Matthiessen, *In the Spirit of Crazy Horse* (New York: Viking, 1991), pp. 130-131.

6. Ibid., p. 260.

7. Ibid., p. 253.

8. Kenneth Stern, Loudhawk: *The United States Versus the American Indian Movement* (Norman, Okla.: University of Oklahoma Press, 1994), p. 73.

Chapter 7

1. Personal statement made by Dennis Banks at the time of his arrest on January 24, 1976, San Francisco, California.

2. Ibid.

3. Kenneth Stern, *Loudhawk: The United States Versus the American Indian Movement* (Norman, Okla.: University of Oklahoma Press, 1994), p. 131.

4. Rex Weyler, *Blood of the Land: The Government and Corporate War Against the American Indian Movement* (New York: Everest House, 1982), p. 209.

5. "Dennis Banks Arrested," *Akwesasne Notes*, Vol. 8, No. 1, 1974, p. 15.

6. Weyler, p. 193.

7. Peter Matthiessen, *In the Spirit of Crazy Horse* (New York: Viking, 1991), p. 264.

8. Stern, p. 159.

9. Letter to Supporters, *The Longest Walk*, Washington, D.C., June 7, 1978.

10. Matthiesen, p. 513.

11. Connie Leslie and Martin Kasindorf, "Dennis Banks's Last Stand," *Newsweek*, February 21, 1983, p. 28.

12. Stern, p. 251.

Chapter 8

1. Fern Malkine, "Interview," *Akwesasne Notes*, Vol. 18, No. 5, 1986, p. 14.

2. Ibid., p. 15.

3. Ibid., p. 14.

4. Ibid.

5. "Sacred Run," Press Release, AIM Field Office, Newport, Ky., June 1995.

6. United Press International, "Traditional Powwow, Emphasizing Sobriety," *The New York Times-National*, January 2, 1994, p. 18.

FURTHER INFORMATION

Books

Blakely, Martha, *Native Americans and the U.S. Government*. New York: Chelsea House, 1995.

Champagne, Duane, ed., (with foreword by Dennis Banks), *Native America: Portrait of the Peoples*. Detroit: Visible Ink Press, 1994.

Crow Dog, Mary, with Richard Erdoes. *Lakota Woman*. New York: Grove Press, 1990.
*Winner of the 1991 American Book Award; later a made-for-television movie on TNN.

Deloria, Vine Jr. *Custer Died for Your Sins: An Indian Manifesto*. New York: The MacMillan Co., 1969

———. *We Talk, You Listen*. New York: MacMillan, 1970.

Hirschfelder, Arlene, and Martha Kreipe de Montaño. *The Native American Almanac: A Portrait of Native America Today*. New York: Prentice Hall General Reference and Travel, 1993.

Niehardt, John (translator). *Black Elk Speaks*. Lincoln, Neb.: University of Nebraska Press, 1979.

Waldham, Carl, with Molly Braun. *Atlas of the North American Indian*. New York: Facts on File, 1985.

Films

The Wounded Knee Affair, 1973, UPI TV News (17 minutes).

Voices from Wounded Knee, by Saul Landau, Institute for Policy Studios, Washington, DC, 1974.

Powwow Highway, Cannon, 1989, Jonathan Wacks, director.

Thunderheart, Columbia Pictures, 1992, Michael Apted, director.

Lakota Woman, Turner Films, 1994, Frank Pierson, director.

⇒ INDEX ⇐

About the
Author

Freelance writer Kae Cheatham has had her poetry and four fiction books published. She is a frequent speaker at schools and churches on the subject of American history. Cheatham travels a lot, photographing and writing articles about rodeos. She shares time at home with two cats, two horses, and a dog.